MY FIRST TRIP TO THE ZOO/ MI PRIMERA VISITA AL ZOOLÓGICO

By Katie Kawa

Traducción al español: Eduardo Alamán

Gareth Stevens
Publishing

Please visit our website, www.garethstevens.com. For a free color catalog of all our high-quality books, call toll free 1-800-542-2595 or fax 1-877-542-2596.

Library of Congress Cataloging-in-Publication Data

Kawa, Katie.
[My first trip to the zoo. Spanish & English]
My first trip to the zoo = Mi primera visita al zoológico / Katie Kawa.
    p. cm. — (My first adventures = Mis primeras aventuras)
Includes index.
ISBN 978-1-4339-6635-4 (library binding)
1. Zoos—Juvenile literature. I. Title. II. Title: Mi primera visita al zoológico.
QL76.K3918 2012
590'.73—dc23

                              2011031661

First Edition

Published in 2012 by
Gareth Stevens Publishing
111 East 14th Street, Suite 349
New York, NY 10003

Editor: Katie Kawa
Designer: Haley W. Harasymiw
Spanish Translation: Eduardo Alamán

All illustrations by Planman Technologies

Printed in the United States of America

CPSIA compliance information: Batch #CW12GS: For further information contact Gareth Stevens, New York, New York at 1-800-542-2595.

Contents

- -

Contenido

Today, I am going to the zoo. I get to see lots of animals!

Hoy, voy al zoológico. ¡Voy a ver muchos animales!

First, we get a map.
This shows us
where the animals are.

Primero, nos dan un
mapa. Así sabemos
donde están los animales.

The animals live
in big houses.
We see them outside too.

Puedo ver como los
cuidadores alimentan
a los animales.

I see workers feeding the animals. They are called zookeepers.

Los cuidadores alimentan a los animales.

I like the elephants.
They use dirt to
stay cool in the sun.

Me gustan los elefantes.
Los elefantes usan tierra
para mantenerse
frescos en el sol.

13

My dad likes the snakes. Glass keeps them from getting out.

A papá le gustan las serpientes. El vidrio evita que las serpientes se salgan.

15

My mom likes the bears. We see brown bears and polar bears.

A mamá le gustan los osos. Vemos osos pardos y osos polares.

I feed a giraffe!
It is tall.

¡Le doy de comer a una
jirafa! Es muy alta.

19

We go to the
petting zoo too.
I pet goats and sheep.

Vamos al zoológico
infantil. Acaricio cabras
y ovejas.

I learned a lot about animals today!

¡Hoy aprendí mucho acerca de los animales!

23

Words to Know/
Palabras que debes saber

glass/
(el) vidrio

map/
(el) mapa

zookeepers/
(los) cuidadores

Index / Índice